Dogs of a Superior

TERRINE GOMEZ

Mayhaven Publishing, Inc.
P O Box 557
Mahomet, IL 61853
USA

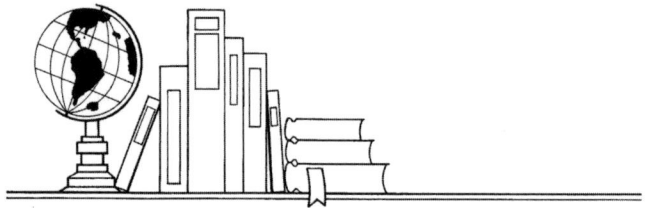

Cover Design: Doris R. Wenzel

Copyright © 2013 Terrine Gomez

First Edition—First Printing 2013

Library of Congress Control Number: 2013939528

ISBN 13: 978 1932278071

❧ Dedication ❧

This book is dedicated to my beloved mama Clara and my sister Tita
who were passionate dog lovers.
And to all my students who love and enjoy them.
Dogs have always given me comfort and security.

Bijou, JouJou, Jascha and Fritz
(sitting on Mama's lap)

I am Bijou. I was born on a farm on June 4, 1992, in At-wood, Illinois. I had two sisters. We were all adopted about the same time. My poor mother must have missed us sorely.

On July 26, 1992, two little old ladies came to our house. They were both very kind to me. I sat on the lap of the older lady, while the younger one drove me to my new house. I was sort of attracted to the driver, and lo and behold, I was happy to find out that she was the one that adopted me.

I was only seven weeks old, and my Mama could hold me in the palm of her hand. Mama took good care of me and I knew I would be happy in my new home. From time to time the other lady used to visit, but then she stopped. We went to visit her one day, and she had a big dog Gigi who was scared of me. I had fun chasing her around the house. Mama named me Bijou, which means Jewel in French. She even bought me a jeweled necklace.

Bijou

Bijou

Mama teaches music — the violin and the viola. At first I was scared, and I still do not like the shrill sounds that some of her students make at their lessons, but some of them are super. All the students know me and I have a lot of fun with them. They baby-sit me when Mama has to leave me for a while. Michelle helped Mama to house-break me. Some very close friends: Sarah, Kirsten, Jennifer, Susan, Audrey, Christine, Eddie, Christopher, David, and Rachel. Sarah's mom and dad took my sisters and me for walks on Saturdays.

Bijou in the backyard

Mama is very strict with me. She is very loving, but very stern. When I get into trouble, she slaps me, but how can I help it when I have no way to get out of the house at night or when Mama forgets to leave some lights on when she leaves the house?

I have good food, but of course I like some of the trash I find outside, especially the little branches. I like to bring them into the house to show off how I can carry things on my own.

By the way, Sam and Fred are my neighbor's dogs. And Charlie is the cat next door. Charlie is scared of me. I love chasing him and the squirrels and I get into trouble again.

At night, I have my own bed, a pillow, my little basket with my two little teddy bears, Mama's old shoes and slippers and a little doggie bone. During the day I have my favorite "blankie," my pet taxi, a ball that jingles and a plastic tug-of-war toy. While Mama teaches, I stay on her desk laying my head on her telephone. When it rings I know she has to talk to somebody.

The second week I was here, Mama's friend Fred came from Europe. I liked him, but Mama would never let me into his room at night. I went with Mama to Chicago to see him off at the airport. Michael Tsay drove us. It was my first long trip in the car. Mama had to smuggle me into a restaurant at the airport while I slept quietly! However, all the passers by thought I was very cute! Mama sent pictures of me to all my friends.

Bijou

Bijou

There is a lot of music in this house, and above all, I enjoy getting to the shoelaces of all my friends. Some like it and others don't. Sometimes I hear the piano next door, but I am not allowed to visit those students.

When Mama went to Minnesota, she left me with some lovely friends in Mahomet, Kara and Erin. There were other dogs, cats, and horses. I even tasted cat food. When Mama came back, she found out that I had too much freedom that whole week, so she started disciplining me in my food and other habits, but I know I am Mama's little baby girl, baby doll, sweetie pie and powder puff. She dotes on me and loads me with love. I live like a princess. My name is Bijou, Mama's Princess Tzu-Hsi, because I come from royal blood. I am also a member of the American Kennel Club. I have had regular trips to the vet doctors Sandra and Pamela. As for Kathy, the secretary, she fusses a lot over me.

I hate baths, but boy, if you know my mama, you have to be clean in this house. Mama also wants me to be a gentle and loving pet to everyone—upstairs and downstairs. My favorite spots are looking out through our windows, waiting for the cars to drive up so I can meet my friends. I have my special place and I do take my naps, there, listening to beautiful music.

Mama sometimes takes me with her in the car. I stay in the car and take a quiet nap while she is busy doing errands.

My mama is very busy, but she has always time for me. She brushes my hair regularly, which I like, and then I play with the brush. We have great times together and I am lucky to be her precious baby.

On January 30, 1993, Mama brought me a big surprise, a little sister — Joujou. She has a French name that means plaything or precious one. She is my toy, she was so small-six-weeks-old, and she hopped from place to place. Her bottom was so large, but as she grew, she became prettier all the time. I had to share all my toys and other stuff with her — and she got more attention from all my friends. I was sort of jealous, but anyway, she was my little baby and I was Mama's baby. We have lots of fun together. Anyway, now when Mama leaves the house, I have company.

Joujou is also a member of the American Kennel Club. Joujou is also known as Princess Tzu-Chin. We have our original names because we come from royal bloodlines. Mama is very particular about having pure-bred dogs.

On June 4, I turned one. Joujou was born on December 17, 1992, at Effingham, Illinois, and Mama went with Mercy to Mattoon to pick her up. Mercy is my good friend. She cooks good food and I just can't wait to have a bite. Rachel, her daughter, loves animals and we can sense that from the way she treats us. Joujou

Joujou and Bijou

Joujou and Bijou

is just six months younger than me. We are very close now — inseparable really. I protect her and Mama in the house. However, Joujou talks too much and she has a high-pitched voice! But she is so petite and so very pretty.

Joujou had her first birthday in December, and we missed seeing our friends during the Christmas vacation. However, winter is fun. We love to play in the snow and collect snowballs on our paws. Mama has a hard time getting rid of those.

Once spring 1994 came, there was a drastic change in the house. We couldn't figure out what was happening. There were boxes all over the place. It disturbed us a great deal because we did not know whether Mama was going to leave us or take us with her to some other place! By late March, Mama's friends Dennis and Marie arrived and their daughters Sarah and Sadie followed a few days later. Sarah could not play with us because of her allergies. We loved this family very much, especially

Marie who took us for very long walks. We always look forward to their visits.

On April 1, 1994, Mama took us to our new home. What a great backyard for Joujou and me to play! There was even a park nearby for our walks. We loved the place. Mama loves the house and she seems very happy and settled now. This dream house is her miracle, she says, thanks to Eleanor, Jon and Marc. Dennis and Marie left after a few days and we miss them, though we know we will see them again.

Mama has informed me that the kind little lady who helped her bring me to Mama, died. I was very sorry to hear this. I wonder what happened to her dog. She always told Mama that she had friends who would take her dog. We hope she was right, because the thought of losing our Mama is very painful.

Finally I met Michele from Indiana. She brought her parents to visit Mama. Her parents live in Brazil. It seems whenever Michele calls here, she always asks about us. That is very sweet of her. So do Marie and Mama's close friends.

Bijou and Joujou

We still love the new place with its great backyard to chase squirrels and birds. Sometimes a rabbit or possum appears. Mama always checks whether the possum is out there in the dark. She doesn't want us to be hurt. The park is a great place too. We meet other dogs, big and small, some wild and some friendly. We made a new friend, Thomas. He comes here often, plays with us and takes us out for walks too. He is a neat guy and we like him a lot.

Guess what? On January 29, 1995, Mama got us a little brother, Jascha, eleven weeks old. He came from Bondville, Illinois. His name is Jascha, Prince Tsu-Chen, and he still has to become a member of the American Kennel Club. It is obvious that he is from royal bloodlines because his very gait proves

Jascha

that. Jascha is cute, very active and adorable. He turned one on November 17ᵗʰ and he wants Joujou and me to play with him all the time. His bark is so loud that at times he is a nuisance.

Maria, who came to clean the house for a while, was very kind and loving to us. Kathy still takes us for baths and medication. Now, Connie cleans the house, and she is also kind. We are lucky to have so many friends and to be loved so well.

Poor Mama was quite ill this winter — we were helpless, but Radha and Steve took care of her and Anita took care of us. We see very little of Ajit, but he is allergic to dogs, we hear. We were happy to see Mama well again and working hard as usual.

In the summer Mama went to Colorado to visit her good friend. We stayed with our lovely friends in Mahomet. We also made friends with Susan Moody at Gibson City. We spent a weekend with her when Mama went to Danville to swear in to become an American Citizen. Later in the summer Michelle came to stay with us for a while. That was super. It was like old times. Her mother is very kind to us, takes us for walks and cleans us. She is a very loving friend.

In the winter of 1996, Mama went to Denmark to visit Annette, her niece. Michelle and Esther took care of us. We were happy to see Mama back on New Years Day. She looked rested and happy. I believe Annette has four dogs, Sam, Honey Bee, Dido and Liu. We would like to meet them, but they live overseas and Mama will not like to torture us in the airplane for hours. Niels is a vet and he loves dogs. It would be lovely if Niels, Annette and Maj visited.

Joujou, Fritz and Bijou

Connie and Maria could not clean the house anymore. We miss them, but Mama found Nikki who loves us. In fact, when Mama had to go to New York twice in the summer for music workshops, we stayed in Nikki's house. She has two children, Sheila and Destiny. Her husband Brandon was also fond of us. Sheila took great care of us. Later on in the summer, Mama had to go to Canada for a whole week. We missed her a lot. I was getting a little edgy and I was mean to the kids. Joujou and Jascha were more composed. We were happy to see Mama again and we hope she stays with us always.

Guess what? Kathy is going to have a baby in December. We are happy for her but we hope she will still fuss over us. She spoils us, and we like that.

The BIG NEWS is that our Michelle is back. When she spends the night here, we sleep with her. She is very patient with us. I am her baby, but she loves Joujou and Jascha too. Jascha is getting to know her and that is nice because Jascha loved Veronica when she was here. He really misses her a lot. Audrey, Albert, Chris and Thayer also visit us. Mama loves to see her students come back to the house, because they are in a way her kids too.

Joujou, Jascha and Bijou

I hear Mama is buying the house. We are happy, because we love it too. The thought of moving again is torture for all of us. Well, on December 23, 1997, Mama bought the house. Now we are all very secure. Mama has her very own place at last and will never move — God willing.

In Spring 2000, Mama got us a cute little brother, Fritz. He was born on January 25, 2000. He had two little teeth sticking out of both ends of his mouth, and when he slept, his tongue stuck out. He is the cutest little fellow and everybody loves him. He plays with Jascha and they can get pretty wild!

Fritz

We had a different vet, Todd Lykins. Gina and Taylor adored us. But suddenly things took a bad turn and we were thrilled to be back with our Dr. Sandra Siwe and Kelly.

They have always taken good care of us and have been very kind to us. We made lots of new friends, Lauren and Jordan. The Haydens took care of us when Mama went to New York in 2001. We miss them, but they visit from time to time.

Jascha, Joujou, Mama
with Fritz, and Bjou

In 2003, Mama returned to New York and Pam, Cheryl and Janna took care of us. Marika loved us all very much.

In January 2003, I was diagnosed as having cancer — palatial squamous cell carcinoma. I met great doctors who tried to help me with radiation, chemotherapy and medication. Thank you, Doctors Weideman, Souza, Hamor and the lovely students who helped us. But in June I got very ill. I had a very special friend, Evan. He came to visit and I felt that I would never see him again. It was a painful experience for me. I sat at his feet and looked up at him, knowing that I might not.

My baby Joujou was also suffering from kidney failure. Mama did all that she could for us. Pam helped her a lot. We are very grateful to all those who helped us in our last days and who we hope will comfort our poor Mama. She will never forget us or stop loving us. Neither will we be away from her for the rest of her life. We hope Jascha and Fritz will give her a lot of happy moments as we tried to do.

Mama decided that Joujou and I had to go together. She arranged for our private cremation on Tuesday, June 10, and our ashes were brought home where we belong. Mama got M.J., another loving friend, to bury the ashes in our favorite backyard near the roses and the shade of the redbud tree. Mama can see our resting place from her bedroom window every morning and evening. Mama thanked us for all the great years we gave her, but she gave us a lovely home with unbelievable comfort and love. Thank you, Mama, and please stop grieving for us for we are free of our aches and pain. God will take care of you and Bijou and Joujou will always be with you. Love you, Mama.

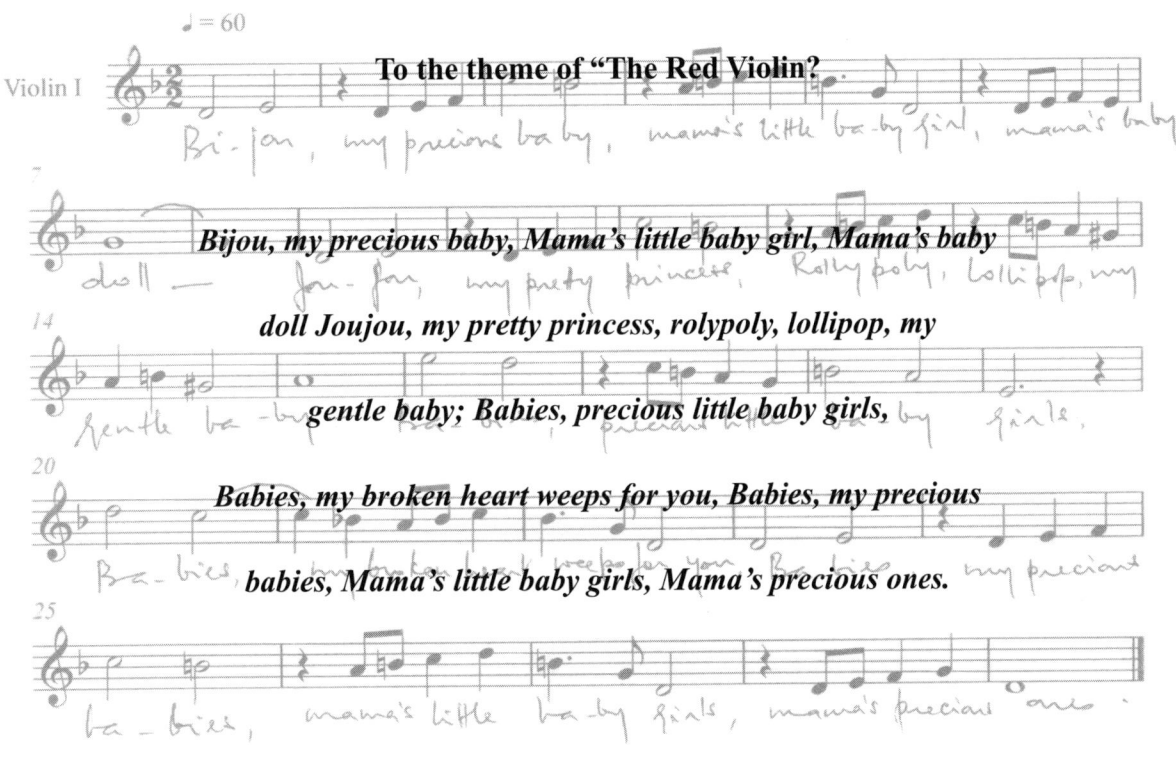

To the theme of "The Red Violin?"

Bijou, my precious baby, Mama's little baby girl, Mama's baby

doll Joujou, my pretty princess, rolypoly, lollipop, my

gentle baby; Babies, precious little baby girls,

Babies, my broken heart weeps for you, Babies, my precious

babies, Mama's little baby girls, Mama's precious ones.

Joujou

My name is Joujou. I was born on December 17, 1992 in Effingham, Illinois. Mama and Mercy came to pick me up at Mattoon. Mercy is a dear friend of ours and so are her children, Nathan and Rachel. Rachel loves animals and I could feel her love for me. I met my older sister Bijou who was very lonely whenever Mama had to go to work or to do errands. So Mama decided to bring me to her home.

I was Mama's pretty princess not only because of my good looks, but I was gentle and soft spoken. I was thoroughly spoiled by every person who came to this house, Mama's students and their parents. I talk too much at times and I have a very high—pitched voice. Bijou tolerated this because I was petite and very pretty.

We always missed seeing our friends during the winter break. But we had fun outdoors. I loved the snow and I used to roll in it and when I came into the house, Mama had a hard time getting rid of those snowballs.

Joujou

Joujou

In 1994, we moved to a lovely neighborhood. The park was near and we had a beautiful backyard. We loved the new house and we were happy and well settled. At first we thought it was not a good idea to move, but once we came here we just loved it. We made lots of friends and there was always a lot of music in this house. There were very young kids and older ones and they all loved us.

Bjou and I have the same vet. Kathy, the secretary who always fussed over me now stays with us when Mama goes on a trip. We bite her ears, tickle her face and jump all over her. We love Kathy because she helps Mama take us to the vet, buy our food and do other countless errands for us.

In 2000, I started putting on a lot of weight and the doctor who took care of me did not check my kidneys. I did not complain so nobody knew the pain I was going through. I was put on a diet which, of course, did not work. However, in 2003, I began to bleed when going to the bathroom. Mama was in New York and Pam took care of me and Bijou, who had already been diagnosed with cancer. When Mama visited me at the hospital, she knew things were getting worse for Bijou and me. We were at the University of Illinois veterinarian school and the doctors were exceptionally kind. They wanted me to have surgery, but because I had only one kidney Mama refused to have this done because she knew I would not survive it. So Mama decided to take us home.

It was a very hard and a sad decision for Mama to have Bijou and me go together. On June 10, Pam took us to our doctor who euthanized us and we were cremated. Our ashes are buried in the backyard of the house.

By this time, Mama had Jascha and Fritz to comfort her. Bijou was her jewel and I was her toy princess.

Mama, thank you for all the love and care, and the music, and all the friends we made. We know
Jascha and Fritz will take care of you.
We love you Mama and all our dear friends. May God take care of you forever.

Bijou, Jascha and Joujou

I am Jascha, born on November 19, 1994, at Bondville. Illinois. My father was Sir Dragon and my mother Dame Ilan. You can see I come from royalty. My grandfather was a show dog. I am always in charge and I am hot-tempered. I do not like to be disturbed when I am sleeping or when I am relaxing in my bed. I have a younger brother Fritz, who joined the family in 2000, and a little sister Titeshka (Petite), who came in 2003. It was hard to adjust to her because I had recently lost my two older sisters, Bijou and Joujou. Bijou was my mama and she was very ill. Joujou was my pretty big sister and she suddenly got very ill and passed away with Bijou on June 10, 2003.

I hear Mama saved Titeshka's life. Another puppy pushed her off a deck by accident and when she came to us she could barely walk on her hind paws. Mama

Jascha

Jascha, Bijou and Joujou

took her to our vet, Dr. Siwe, who got her growing strong and well. Fritz and Titeshka have the same father, so they get along very well and they play a lot together, but she loves me too and showers me with kisses whenever she can.

I am Mama's handsome boy, and I have some good friends. Some kids are scared of me because of my temper. Mama takes good care of the three of us. My back hurts because of a disc problem. I also have arthritis like Mama. When I am hurting, Mama sends me to the vet and I get a shot and some pills to ease my pain.

In 2005, Mama had to have her knees replaced, because she couldn't bear the pain anymore. Doctor Robert Bane helped her and she is up and moving a lot easier. Our friend Pamela took care of us both times. The left knee surgery was in March 2005 and the right-knee surgery was in December of the same year. Carolyn took care of us and she took care of Mama when she came home to recover. Our good friend Becky took Mama regularly to therapy sessions, which were very painful. She also took her, most of the time, to Mama's doctor visits.

Usually I sleep in my basket at night, but now I like to keep Mama's legs warm because she gets cold at night. Fritz is jealous that I have taken his place. He acts up from time to time, but he is now quite used to the routine. Titeshka has her comfortable little bed, but now she is acting grown up and tries to be independent. Mama has a bad cough and Fritz doesn't like the sound of it. Tite (a pet name for Titeshka) and I got used to it. We want Mama to stay well and healthy.

Monika helps Mama and she loves us a lot. She takes us out for a walk before she works. Our good friend Deb feeds us and takes us out for walks most of the days of the week. We love her and we know she loves us. Maria visits us sometimes on Sundays, and spoils us with treats. Then she gives us a good bath and makes sure we are clean before she leaves. We have known her for a very long time even when our older sisters, Bijou and Joujou, were alive. Mama gives us some turkey or beef slices for lunch and some hard food. Then in the evening we get our soft food. I bug all the students and parents for treats and Mama does not like that, so we get very little. I suppose that's good for our health.

In 2006, Mama had her cataracts removed, the left eye in September and the right eye in October. Her sight has improved.

In 2007, Mama decided to go to Memphis in the spring, once to visit Cleophas and his family and another time to meet Jerome who is a doctor. By the way, Jerome helped Mama with her cough and it is almost gone. I hope he'll continue to take good care of Mama.

Mama went to Europe in the summer. Rachel, our dear old friend, along with Monica, Carolyn, Catherine, Caitlin and Deb helped us. We missed Mama, especially Fritz, but we knew she would be back soon. She always comes back. Rachel went back to London and Monica left, too. Monica's Danny got a good job in Boston and they moved. We miss her a lot. She helped Mama and Mama misses her sorely. Peggy comes to clean. She is nice but not as warm as our other friends. Maria comes once in a while.

A lovely Korean family came a year ago and thankfully decided to stay another year. They were kind to Mama and to us. Yooyi and Alex were wonderful. Alex is my friend. We loved each other very much. They fed us and took us for long walks. We will miss them when they leave.

Recently, I scared Mama when I couldn't sleep because I was having trouble breathing through the whole night. I went to Dr. Siwe the next morning and Mama was told that I had an enlarged heart and fluid in my lungs. Mama and all my friends were devastated. With medication and proper diet, I felt much better. I turned 14 on November 19, 2008. That is pretty old, but I stay young at heart with all the love I get from Mama and my friends, and Fritz and Tite. Unfortunately, feeling good only lasted for a few days and on December 5, I got very ill. My breathing got worse and I was very restless. When Daniel came to his lesson, he noticed that I was restless and was quite worried about me. He is a very special friend of all of us. Later that evening when Juliana took me outside after her lesson, she was also painfully aware that I was very weak. Mama put me on her bed to soothe me, but I coughed up blood and I breathed my last. Dr. Welle and Julia took me to their clinic before informing Dr. Siwe. It was the weekend and Dr. Siwe and our friend Kelly were not available. Mama took good care of me during my last hours and finally I passed away.

I know this made Mama very sad and heart-broken. I was her handsome boy, her very special boy and she had pet names for me that I loved to hear: Monni, Monnino, Manno and Mamunni. Fritz and Tite will also miss me, but I am happy they are still there to take care of my mama. And I am happy to have joined my sisters Bijou and Joujou.

Mama,

I love you and thank you for taking care of me for 14 years. I felt like a puppy all the time and I loved playing with all my toys. I loved the music in this house and all my young friends. God will take care of you Mama.

Love you, Mama.

May Fritz and Titeshka comfort you and love you.

Jascha

Bijou, Fritz, Jascha and Joujou

Fritz

❧ Fritz ❧

I am Fritz, born on January 24, 2000 in Tolono, Illinois. Mama visited my home and when I was eight weeks old, I was ready to go to Mama's house. She liked my dad, Dafu, and she says I inherited his affectionate ways.

In Mama's house there were already two girls and a boy. Bijou, Joujou and Jascha. Bijou was a mother to me. Joujou was just my pretty sister and Jascha was my playmate. We had a lot of fun together. However, in 2003, I lost Bijou and Joujou. Bijou had cancer and Joujou had a kidney problem. Jascha and I were very sad and so was Mama. That year Mama was asked to save the life of a miniature sister of ours, Titeshka (Petite). She was hurt by one of her siblings and she could not walk on her hind paws. Her spine was injured and she needed special care and help. Our good Dr. Siwe took care of her and she grew stronger all the time. She was also Dafu's baby and that brought us very close to each other. She was eight and a half years old when suddenly she lost a lot of weight and got weaker. Dr. Siwe detected some lumps on her and with antibiotics she was cured. But unfortunately she had to go back to the doctor and the xray showed a lump in her chest. She was too frail and too little to undergo surgery. We lost her, and Mama and I were heartbroken.

Now I have a new little friend Mischa. He was born on August 2, 2011. He is Jascha's half brother. It was difficult to get used to him at first. He is wild and chews wood, books and almost anything he can find. Sometimes he chews my ear so hard and my tail that it hurts. I know he is being playful, but it is not fun for me. Otherwise we have a lot of fun playing together. He was only eight weeks old when he came to us. He is growing fast and climbs up to pull objects down, like the remote control. He likes to hide under all the couches, and play peek–a–boo. I was pretty lonely and sad when Tite left us, so in a way it was good to have Mischa in the house. He sleeps in a crate at night and that is when Mama and I can spend some quality time. I can't wait for him to calm down, hopefully that might happen when he has all his teeth and it will be wonderful if he stops chewing anything and everything he can find.

Mischa is very handsome and reminds me of my Jascha. I feel younger and happier now. I am twelve years old and I have a heart problem. I have to be medicated for the rest of my life. However, Mischa

Mischa

is fun and keeps me going.

When I turned 13, on January 24, 2013, I was diagnosed with kidney problems in addition to my weak heart. Mama took very special care of me. I had a hard time eating any food. Petra, another friend of mine. tried to coax me to eat some food. Deb visited and she was also concerned about me. Finally, on March 8, I passed blood and that made my mama very worried and sad. She realized the end was near. I know Mischa will take care of her, but I know my mama will miss me forever. I was her Fritza, her Fritzi, her Fritzmo, her Puppy, her friend and companion. I wanted her always with me.

Mischa

I am grateful to Dr. Sandra Siwe, my wonderful vet, and Kelly who came faithfully to take us for our medical needs, food included. To Dr. Mary Welle, who always helped us through her daughter Julia, Aja, Bokeum, Patrick, especially when they knew I was getting weaker. Patrick's dad Richard helps us a lot when he has the time. My heart is filled with thanks to all my friends.

When my older friends, Mama's former students visited her, they made me feel so good and loved. Nathan Wells and his sister Rachel, Daniel Borup, Linda Song, Caroline Roloff, Anthony Williams, David Lisker and many others. Even their families loved me. It was nice to be loved and taken care of in a home filled with beautiful live music, good food and surrounded by loving friends, especially my beloved mama.

Fritz, my friend and my companion
My Liebesfreud, alive in my heart
You are now my Liebesleid,
Always a gentleman, a thoroughbred
Goodbye my precious Puppy!

My name is Titeshka. I was born in Tolono on January 9, 2003. I am a miniature Shih Tzu. One of my siblings pushed me down a slope and I injured my spine and I could not walk on my hind paws. My breeder was looking for a good home and a kind soul to take care of me because she could neither sell me nor have the heart to put me down. On July 12, 2003, I was taken to the home of a very warm and sweet lady. She had just lost Bijou and Joujou, two of her female dogs and had only two male dogs surviving, Jascha and Fritz. The lady became my Mama who took exceptional care of me — got me cured of my problems and I grew stronger and stronger day by day.

Dr. Sandra Siwe was my vet. She was very good and caring. Her assistant Kelly Cotter always took us to our

Jascha, Titeshka and Fritz

vet when we needed medical help. Dr. Mary Welle, whose daughter Julia is Mama's violin student, helped me a lot along the way.

As for our groomer Janice, she adored me and even gave me a jeweled collar and lots of toys for all of us. Debra Medlyn is another great friend of ours who took us for walks. If she saw I was tired, she would carry me in her arms, lovingly, and take care of me. I hated extremely cold or extremely hot weather. Deb loved us and always came faithfully to feed us and give us a good walk.

People thought I was cute because I was always so petite in spite of getting on in years. Mama teaches music and all her students and their parents loved me and literally spoiled me.

Then sadly, on December 5, 2008, my brother Jascha died of fluid in his lungs and an enlarged heart. He was very handsome and I adored him. He had a short temper, probably due to his illness. We were all sad when he left us and we still miss him.

I was happy to learn that Fritz was my half brother. We had the same father. Fritz bugged me a lot. He liked to jump on me, and oh boy, he was so heavy! I bullied him too sometimes. Can you imagine my life with two big strong boys?

Anyway, I started losing weight suddenly and my vet discovered lumps under my chin and on the shoulder. The tests showed that they were not cancerous. But I continued losing weight and on June 24, 2011, Mama sent me to my vet. She called Mama to let her know that I had a tumor in my chest and that I was too small and too weak to undergo surgery. Mama got me home immediately to love me and help me survive. But the next day, June 25, I started having convulsions and seizures and that was the sign that I was nearing the end. Dr. Welle and Julia took me for my last rites. Mama was devastated.

Mama and Fritz and all my friends in Mama's studio will miss me, especially my Melody who carried me around like a baby! Anthony was another favorite of mine. He used to take us for walks whenever Mama needed him.

Thank you Mama for all the love and care you gave me. Fritz will take care of you, but then, — he is always begging for food!

Rachel and Titeshka

Mischa

I, Mischa, was born on August 2, 2011. I was taken to a beautiful home where there was an old loving dog, Fritz. He had recently lost his miniature half-sister Titeshka and he was very sad and lonely. I liked Fritz, but I was not sure if he was ready to have me as his little brother. I was Jascha's half-brother and, I thought, definitely made it easier for him to accept me. I am named Mischa after the great violinist Mischa Elman. Fritz was named after Fritz Kreisler and Jascha after Jascha Heifetz, all of them were great violinists. I am Mama's Mischa!

My mama teaches music, the violin and the viola, and there are always students and their parents visiting. I am the center of attraction. They find me cute, but wild! Well, I am still a puppy and I am busy exploring places and things. Students are of all ages. Emily is six, loves me very much. When Juliana came to her music lesson, the first day I was in my new home, she was very surprised to see me. Her mother immediately brought me gifts and they spoiled me. Melody adores me and the feeling is mutual. I went to her home on Christmas

Fritz, Juliana, holding Titeshka, and Jascha

Day when Mama had to be with friends who had a dog in their home. Jeremiah loves me very much, but I haven't seen him for awhile. I hope he is well and will visit soon. Barbara, Mama's friend, also babysits me when Mama calls her for help. Kathleen, Allison and Julia spoil me a lot, too. Julia's mother, Dr. Mary Welle, keeps an eye on me and I have been to their home. She is a vet and is very helpful to Mama.

I have this bad habit of chewing anything and everything I see, particularly good wood. When Patrick's dad visits, he gives me keys to chew on and he doesn't even mind me chewing the laces on his shoes. Another problem for Mama is that I have to be taken out with a leash because I tend to chew everything I see in the yard. That is tough in the winter, especially when we are having a long winter. Melody tries to get me out of this bad habit.

On Saturdays, the students come for chamber music rehearsals. I have to sit in my kennel and listen to them because if I am allowed to walk around to greet my friends, I would be tempted to chew their instruments, which are all made of good wood. What a treat that would have been for me!

In March 2013, I lost my loving brother Fritz. He was sick with heart and kidney problems. Puppy that I was, I gave him a rough time chasing him around, chewing his ear and pulling his tail. It was fun and play for me, and I did not realize that I was hurting him. It is sad that he is not here anymore. I was told that he has gone home and I had to take care of Mama. Anthony comes to walk me most evenings. I wait for him to feed me and then he takes me for a long walk before I got to bed. Patrick is also very kind to me. At night I sleep in my kennel with my toys, my pillow and comfortable blankies to keep me warm.

Occasionally, I look up to see if my mama is still reading or sleeping in her bed.

I am a lucky dog and I hope I'll have many more years with my mama and all my dear friends. Thank you, Mama, for a beautiful home, lovely music, good food and loving friends. I will try to be a good boy and a wonderful companion!

Fritz and Bijou

Anleen and her mother, with Mischa and Fritz

Mischa and Fritz at play

Mischa and Fritz still at play

Melody with Titeshka and Kathleen with Fritz

Mischa in
his bed

Julia with Mischa

Allison and Mischa

Jascha

Joujou, Bijou, Jascha and Fritz

Joujou, Jascha and Bijou

Bokyo and Bokeuom
with Fritz

Mischa and Kate

Mischa and Juliana

Fritz and Mischa under the piano

Aja with Mischa

Jeremiah and Enoch with Fritz and Mischa

Anura and Mischa

Titeshka and Fritz

Mischa and Melody

Mama teaching Sarah